Special Days

Weddings Around the World

by Emily C. Dawson

amicus
readers

1

Amicus Readers are published by Amicus
P.O. Box 1329, Mankato, Minnesota 56002

Copyright © 2011 Amicus. International copyright reserved in all
countries. No part of this book may be reproduced in any form
without written permission from the publisher.

Printed in the United States of America at Corporate Graphics,
North Mankato, Minnesota.

Library of Congress Cataloging-in-Publication Data
Dawson, Emily C.
  Weddings around the world / by Emily C. Dawson.
      p. cm. – (Amicus readers. Special days)
  Includes index.
  Summary: "Describes and compares different wedding customs
around the world. Includes simple craft"–Provided by publisher.
  ISBN 978-1-60753-031-2 (library binding)
  1. Marriage customs and rites–Juvenile literature. 2. Weddings–
Juvenile literature. I. Title.
  GT2690.D39 2011
  395.2'209–dc22

                                                    2010010553

Series Editor   Rebecca Glaser
Series Designer   Emily Brown
Book Designer   Heather Dreisbach
Photo Researcher   Heather Dreisbach

Photo Credits
ALEXANDER JOE/Staff/Getty Images, 9; Corbis, 15, 17, 20
(m); Corbis/Tranz, 7, 12, 13, 21 (t); Ctacik/Dreamstime.com,
10; Devinder Sangha/Alamy, 11, 20 (b); Digital Vision, 14,
21 (m); Gregory Wrona/Alamy, 19; Lacy Rane/iStockphoto, 3,
20–24 (roses); Peter Treanor/Alamy, cover; Photodisc, 1, 21 (b);
SuperStock/Alamy, 5, 20 (t); Tamera Rees/iStockphoto, 4

1225
42010

10 9 8 7 6 5 4 3 2 1

Table of Contents

A wedding is when two people get married.

The woman who gets married is the bride. The man who gets married is the groom.

groom

bride

5

Weddings are different around the world.

In India, the bride and groom walk around a fire.

7

In South Africa,
some people have
mass weddings.

Many couples
get married at
the same time.

In many places,
brides and grooms
give each other rings.

Wedding rings are
a symbol that love
will last forever.

**wedding
ring** ◄

Brides and grooms wear fancy clothes.

In Indonesia, the bride wears a gold headdress. The groom wears a cloth cap.

headdress

In Mexico, brides wear a white veil and dress.

The groom also wears white.

veil ←⋯

After weddings, people have a special meal.

In America, many couples have a wedding cake with layers.

Many people have parties after weddings.

This couple in Romania has a wedding dance.

The guests dance too.

19

Picture Glossary

bride
a woman who is about to get married

couple
two people who are in love with each other; they may get married.

groom
a man who is about to get married

headdress

a decorative
covering for
the head

veil

a covering for the
head or face worn
by a woman

wedding

a ceremony when
two people get
married; they
promise to live
their lives together.

21

Make a Wedding Gift

Guests bring gifts for the wedding couple. A picture frame makes a nice gift.

Supplies:

- Plain wooden picture frame
- Buttons, shells, or sequins
- Glue
- Wrapping paper or gift bag

1. Choose buttons, shells, or sequins in the bride's favorite color.

2. Glue the decorations onto the picture frame. Let dry.

3. Wrap the gift and bring it to the wedding.

Ideas for Parents and Teachers

Special Days, an Amicus Readers Level 1 series, gives children practice reading about real-life celebrations they will likely encounter. The picture glossary reinforces new vocabulary. The activities give children a chance to link ideas from the book to their own lives. Use the ideas listed below to help children get even more out of their reading experience.

Before Reading:
- Ask the students if they have ever been to a wedding. Ask them to tell the group what the wedding was like.
- Read the title and have the students talk about the cover photo. Does it look similar to a wedding they have been to or seen?

Read the Book:
- Read the book to the children or have them read independently.
- Show children how to use the features of the book such as the photo labels and picture glossary.

After Reading:
- Make a similarities and differences chart about weddings around the world.
- Talk to the students about things that are special at weddings. Prompt them with questions, such as *What do some brides wear on their heads? Why is a cake at some weddings?*

23

Index

Web Sites

Africa People and Culture—Wedding Ceremonies
http://www.africaguide.com/culture/weddings.htm

Indian Wedding Rituals
http://www.culturalindia.net/weddings/wedding-rituals/index.html